HOSTS AND GUESTS

PRINCETON SERIES OF CONTEMPORARY POETS

Susan Stewart, series editor

For other titles in the Princeton Series of Contemporary Poets, see page 83.

HOSTS AND GUESTS

Poems

Nate Klug

PRINCETON UNIVERSITY PRESS
Princeton and Oxford

Requests for permission to reproduce material from this work
should be sent to permissions@press.princeton.edu

Published by Princeton University Press
41 William Street, Princeton, New Jersey 08540
6 Oxford Street, Woodstock, Oxfordshire OX20 1TR

press.princeton.edu

Library of Congress Cataloging-in-Publication Data
Names: Klug, Nate, 1985- author.
Title: Hosts and guests : poems / Nate Klug.
Description: 1st. | Princeton, New Jersey : Princeton University Press,
    [2020] | Series: Princeton series of contemporary poets | Includes
    bibliographical references and index.
Identifiers: LCCN 2020002306 (print) | LCCN 2020002307 (ebook) | ISBN
    9780691203546 (hardback) | ISBN 9780691203539 (paperback) | ISBN
    9780691203553 (ebook)
Subjects: LCGFT: Poetry.
Classification: LCC PS3611.L82 H67 2020 (print) | LCC PS3611.L82
(ebook)
    | DDC 811/.6—dc23
LC record available at https://lccn.loc.gov/2020002306
LC ebook record available at https://lccn.loc.gov/2020002307

British Library Cataloging-in-Publication Data is available

Editorial: Anne Savarese and Jenny Tan
Production Editorial: Ellen Foos
Text Design: Pamela Schnitter
Jacket/Cover Design: Pamela Schnitter
Production: Erin Suydam
Copyeditor: Jodi Beder

Jacket art: Joan Brown, *St. Francis and St. Claire*, 1989. Oil on canvas,
96 × 78 inches. © The Estate of Joan Brown. Image courtesy of
George Adams Gallery, New York. Photo © 2017, J. Jones

This book has been composed in Adobe Garamond Pro

Printed on acid-free paper. ∞

Printed in the United States of America

10 9 8 7 6 5 4 3 2 1

FOR KIT

We love we know not what: and therefore everything allures us.

—Thomas Traherne

Contents

4

HOSTS AND GUESTS

1.

MATINEE, END OF AUGUST

The several dark
where it was safe to feel

still wearing off our faces,
we stumble out
with packs of strangers

like red-eye passengers
exiting a jet,
crumbs and random warmths
scattered among the recliner seats.

The future, like a memory,
seeps back slowly:

which car, which color-coded floor . . .
It ought to have rained.
We'd wanted not to hurry.
But every door

to the reassembling world
knows we're there already,
and slides open.

GHOST AT THE HY-VEE

I'd seen him just two months before—
his brother's service, condolences
over orange juice—but when I shook Dan's hand

between aisles, my lips spoke "Jack."
Or Jack spoke "Jack" through me, slipping back
by vowel rhyme, and scrambling to remain

among the glint and friction of the jumbo carts,
midday's automatic produce mists. Cheeks drained,
then flushed, believing too much at once

to speak, I glanced toward Dan, his eyes
fixed below on the ceiling fans' reflections—
each circulating blade leaking up

through floor varnish. Returned to himself,
he laughed it off, clapping my back like a man,
like a Dan would, but more softly than that.

CHRISTMAS EVE, I-80, 10 P.M.

Tipped and stranded and sheathed in snow,
        adjacent the rumble strip
a semi-trailer slumbers through
        its own decomposing.
Tied with a skinny orange ribbon,

it'll lie there how long, a sea creature's
        bleached inchoate bones
risen among the prairie's ambered forms
        and beached on an interstate ditch?
Once, an enormous seaway

ran straight through this country,
        flattened a plate and filled six hundred miles
in the middle—a wide shallow avenue
        seething with animals:
picture them for company in the dark,

plesiosaurs and clam-eating sharks
        and the shifting bell curves of plankton
all thronging here, between Altoona
        and The Lion's Den, its lurid neon sign
newly redone, store lights still on.

HOSTS AND GUESTS

After the ID forgotten en route,
the forced deplaning thanks
to fog reports, after three thousand miles

of bladder vs. historical thriller—"still,
all in all, easier than getting to Des Moines"—
here they are again, though they've never been,

perched either side of our mutt
at the linty edge of the same turquoise couch.
What could we offer to repay them?

Stuffed into East Coast coats, they paw
through carry-on Kleenex, hand over a folder
of direct mail addressed to us,

interrupt to show off a new app.
Their love an ebullition
of non sequiturs and questions

fired past any chance of a response,
while you and I slip back
into randomly specific irritations,

equally unable to help ourselves.
It's like that time we gathered to watch
an old family VHS—

the coloring a little off almost immediately,
your yellow bucket hat bleeding
into your toddler head, merging it with other heads,

while everyone on screen around you
in the kitchen laughed and cooed,
the merging getting worse the longer we tried

to keep the movie playing.
A week later, airport location
loaded on both their phones, after long hugs

goodbye (your father and I
finished first, stood looking at the sky
for several seconds), how empty

now our new apartment feels,
ransacked of their shadows, smells,
each familiar gesture's weight. Straightening up,

we walk each room hand in hand—relieved,
but fighting off an unexpected grief,
alone as if for the first time.

EYE OF A NEEDLE

Mountain View Cemetery, Oakland

Hard to tell the mourners from the exercisers,
heads down as they fan out
from the parking circle, pistoning steep paths
beyond the columbaria,
Rihanna maybe hidden in one hand.
An open book, slab pages uncut;
a few cherubs, in need of a wash,
among the headstone crescents—then the mausoleums,
higher up that same crest, each a little country jail
sheltering the nineteenth-century
smelting families, Navy admirals, barons
of Folgers coffee. Poor Wintermute,
once hung with a *For Sale* sign,
though who could blame the grandson?
Ghirardelli with his bar of chocolate
tucked in a fresh fake wreath at every season.
One wickless candle, if there's an altar
inside, plastic roses facing a bench
for nobody to sit on, and a painted pasture
in the opalescent window, usually
a pane or two gouged out.
New locks on some door grates
as though they'd guessed we look.
Sensing rain, carpenter ants

funnel up the same granite slab my friend would lean against
like its animated grains.
They thin to single file within the shelter
of carved letters, revising a hook to a ligature,
busy at their lip of space.

JUBILEE

In Day-Glo vest, delicate
      among the sidewalk's children,
each Tuesday morning
      hopping off here, he taps
the side loader joystick up,
      looking on, looking nowhere
as the claw lowers, pincers
      fasten around the curb's
first bin. *Count seven sabbaths*
      of years; count seven times
those seven. On the tenth
      day of that seventh month,
proclaim freedom; return
      each man to his possession.

Lid flapping open, the bin tips,
      shakes a liquid sequence
toward the iron bed's throat
      then drops, released,
to knock against the next,
      stirring a ragged confetti
of wrappers and scratch tickets.
      He's already twisted

so half his torso hangs
      inside the cab, when the truck
jumps, without signaling,
      back into traffic, the astonished
horns not yet transformed
      to shofar trumpets.

OURSELVES

Digging at Half-Moon Bay,
the dog dreams too hard—

a rattle of tags
near our legs in bed,

and sleep's last sneaker
wave breaks. All the way

until speaking, lying here,
you and I might

lay waste to or create anything,
little tyrants without names

passing pasts between each other.
But day's first words

arrive like nets, flung
from somewhere behind

our heads. We can hear the worn
rigging catch, involuntary

as animal muscle,
assuring us who we are—

rooted, fooled,
to this side of the shore.

REV. VALENTINE RATHBUN
MEETS THE SHAKERS

Niskayuna, New York, 1780

Whose throat did it start from,
the tune that tests the length
of the wooden, high-windowed room,
an unknown mutter mixed with English
sliding like static
among their prone spirits
until, without apparent sign
or rule, all fall in,
dancing, hopping,
the Believers bound together
only in their bodies'
tensions, their coiled
distinctions from each other:
one jigs, one drops face-first to the floor,
one blends to the wall in prayer,
one stands and claps,
defiantly bored.
Wind fills the fastest dresses,
sprays them up, like toy hoops,
when the Mother changes time,
rapping out the new notes.
"This the company calls

the worship of God, which stops
oddly as it began,
and one by one
they break off, trailing laughter,
for a spell of smoking."

THE CONVERT (I)

Stars burn away
of their own vivid weight
or turn to pins
that must've, all along, been planes

as faces, cooled
by the years, or taught fear late,
might crease near the eyes
tendering ambition's mistakes

but my sculling mind
determined to go back
to believe in nothing
finds it can't—at sea, in faith

GREAT BLUE HERON, SPOFFORD LAKE

One thing to do
until you can't
is wait, foot tentative
testing for deceit

as if aligned
with some superior quiet
there at the ice's edge

as chimneys pulse
on a little ledge above
and a plasma screen
gutters, mistaken for a living room fire
across the lake

Dolled up gunmetal
still as a mime
you balance, oblivious
contemptuous

of audience
and elaborating well
into the night your small

dangerous
adjustments

LION'S MANE JELLYFISH

Encased along the Sound
like little Jeff Koons basketballs,

they never seem to move, but multiply.
I swam every afternoon, before I knew.

Wading in and about to dive,
a neighbor saw one toppling along the bottom,

tipped on its side, tissue
streaming from the Gorgon mouth, or back.

Having no center sustained it? That weekend
they'd clustered in the harbor,

confused, I was told later,
by the temperature (if one can be confused

without a heart, or brain).
Dark enough, the surface hid

their moons and toxic manes.
If you want to remember your dreams,

my father said, *remind*
yourself, right before you fall asleep.

Concentrate; but go to sleep.
All September, I hadn't spotted any

until one morning I found
too many, flaking gray like sick lilies,

tide-sloshed against the embankment stones.
Or was it, looking back,

that they'd come for me already
in lack of feeling, in the cloud fleets

after sunset, drooping and translucent,
I could skewer my finger through, but never touch?

2.

THE OUTDOOR AMPITHEATER
AT ASHWORTH PARK

Only one kind
of life would think

to lie down

loudly in the middle
of this leafless

whiteness

in such wind, scraping
arms and legs

back and forth—

herald angel/
distress signal—

and yelling for its partner

to take its picture,
another

ACONITE

What's bane to wolves and whales
and poisons humans
nourishes the dot moth
and the yellow-tailed,

the wormwood pug, as dark
as a slug, the nervous
mouse moth, and the engrailed.
Distinguish milk-white

from ivory, learn to locate
sepals of aconite
from the trail: they resemble devils'
helmets one day

and, the next, the delicate cowls
Dominicans adjust
in prayer. No single appellation
fits, but, like a magnet,

pushes toward its opposite.
When the three-jawed dog
landed here, snarling at the sun
and pining for Hades,

his rabid sounds scattered
white foam,
drool which took root in Scythia
but flourished in areas

of higher rock, crag peaks
where nothing useful
bloomed, and no dust reached.
Now, down-creeping

into clearings, stalks wavering
along the tracks
that once linked factory towns,
the flower's grown

as inexorable as speech—
sustenance
or toxin, to anyone
who wanders close.

BOSTON POST ROAD

I'm in her front seat heading home from school,
a stranger's car, a family friend's best friend,

it having been told to me in a hurry
early that morning that she'd know the way,

with something stumbling in their explaining
which told me too how, just like that, I could be lost,

so when we pass the familiar turn the moment
doesn't even happen fast, and the longer now I wait to speak

the farther away we're getting, the farther back
both of us would have to go, and so I don't

because construction, or a detour, the driver
armed with reasons I would understand but can't,

or probably I never paid enough attention
to these dark town greens and peeling steeples in the past

and we're right on course, judging by her humming
and chat, home in time to sneak TV, or fumble through

a few drawers upstairs, before the others return
with their kind tired voices, their sounds for my name.

WATER CLOCKS

To slow down panic on planes
        or just before sleep,
think back, if you can,
        to the work of water clocks:
how a toothed wheel, nudged
        by falling drops, would rotate,
rectify the dial,
        and in that way an hour,
felt or not, was proved;

        or else floating rods
that counted as they pointed,
        shaky, jiggered higher
while their pewter basins filled,
        the kind of time implied
neither reversible
        nor self-contained (like sand
in glass)—more credible,
        treating forms as vessels
meant to be escaped:

        the same tenuous machines
which Pompey ordered placed
        in every court, to better
calibrate the people's speech,

   though in three years he'd flee,
still proud, but old now, stabbed
    in the midst of standing up,
his small boat almost
    all the way to Egypt.

APORIA

Not little by little,

as concerto strings
or doctrines like

to disappear,

leaving time
to think. No—skin

still tensed around

jaw and powdered cheek,
seen from the side

in the sea of the bed:

none now
that was her is there.

JASPER COUNTY ALMANAC

1. October

Three orange vests against sage grass.
And the duct-taped scope
the skinny one steadies

on a rotted stake—
same break in the ditch wire

where, at dusk, on the other end
of work, bucks scour
the wind for urine scents,

heads rearing at each swerving
of our flicked-on brights.

2. April

Rain's prediction means
more topsoil, slopped as soon
as possible into the local gullies

to jostle with earlier stormwater
so that, driven down

any hint of a track,
PK fertilizers pull
from surface sheets

and, in ditches a farm or two
away, the mixture blooms

as blue-green algae's
galactic swirls. Slinks
toward public drains.

POTHOLES

Though chipped and complex
      as oak knots, when potholes
saturate with rain they resolve
      to a black unbroken sheen—
like hundreds of filings
      pulled flat, magnetized—
and messenger bikes get but a second

      to swerve. Rapt in a billboard
tickered with real-time quotes
      or levels of alert, the rider
snaps his head back
      to the erratic ground itself,
to the chance of the Earth's
      opening up, blasting
through macadam and dirt
      these chest-wide trapdoors

which might, for all he can see,
      just keep going down:
Buster Keaton, Yellow Wolf,
      and that ferryman's dog,
all two hundred and fifty
      enemies of Moses, swallowed
by God. Or else, it's worse,

the deepest pits on Market Street
exist to light the way back up
        for every narrative
we've paved and girded over
        or never even learned,
the jealous limbs reaching
        toward the surface breaches . . .

IMPATIENT EARTH

after Horace

Snows scatter, and leaves, soon after,
swarm back to their trees, netted all at once
like Indiana bats. The errant circuit
of the moon's made up for what it spent;
too fast now, grass will resume
the awkward berms along the canal
and abandoned armory lawns. Stooped
among spider webs in a municipal garage,
Vosburgs Jr. and Sr. test the intentions
of pull cords, in their heads the weeds
rampant already . . .
              Isn't it soon to say
how long your heart's change will last,
or by what terms—though we leave them belief,
a little eloquence—descendants might speak
of a devoured Earth? Years after the accident,
Diana still dreams she sees her friend,
while tenacious Theseus may never catch
the voice of King Pirithous, hard once
though he loved him, far as he reaches back.

BROOD III

Sap suffices for their time
     in the dark, tapped, syringe-wise,
straight to their brains
       from coiled plant roots;
   we've no desire

with which to compare
     that seething breach of the Earth
after seventeen years,
    receiving air, sun,
       all at once, then feeling
toward shrub or sapling trunk.
    A nymph's shell
splits down the back

    and in an hour the adult's out—
Mars-red toggle-eyes
    and vellum wings—to mate
      and hide its eggs
in the linings of twigs,
   before dying
belly up, just the size
    of a child's watch face.

A periodical cicada's legs
    might still seem
to paddle, landed for good on sidewalks
            and country club lawns
among the earlier
    discarded skins

mowers (over the males' sound)
    can only spit back,
re-scatter: sequined
            exoskeletons
remembered mainly
    for plaguing wedding season.

"GRACE IS STILL A SECRET"

Not that anyone actually changes—that the small charge
of a green change can't help but stumble,

on its own time, among no particular
people, feeling nothing, nothing different,

close faces on the L craning toward another's phone
or, alone, toward some point through the glass at track's end

perhaps, in the dark the unstill ground
hiding and giving us where we are going.

FOR OUR ANNIVERSARY IN EARLY JUNE

Fireflies   a few peonies
after rain the same week

faint as one another
as again they start

from the shyness of near dark
still needing it   to be seen

THE POKÉMON GO PEOPLE

Not pretending to be shopping,
they canvass cobblestoned Water Street, nearsighted
as beach sweepers, their devices feeling ahead
for which alleyway, or corner of a yard,
might sprout a Snorlax, a purple Aerodactyl.

"These are the Pokémon Go people," explains a villager
to her guest, careful not to point as one group passes,
their jean shorts to mid-shin, arms arabesqued
with dates or skewered hearts, some steering strollers.

Scattered among the eighteenth-century colonials,
the Improvement Association's clapboard plaques
remember Hale, ship captain, and Stewart, joiner,
each calling stenciled right beneath the name.
In this new life, vocation's not so certain—

assignments can vibrate at any time, the location
of a needed creature flash, then disappear.
You almost have to be waiting there already,
disconsolate after a day of nothing
as light drains at the former hotspot in Cannon Square.

When two wild Pikachu clamber
over the rocks, the woman shrieks and punches her partner,
to make sure he'd seen. A postcoital quiet
on their drive back home to Pawcatuck.

3.

FIRST LENT IN CALIFORNIA

A face not fearing light —George Herbert

Californians need to do a thing to enjoy it —James Schuyler

1.

Caused perhaps by the constant
sunlight, our dog has developed a cutaneous horn.
"Don't Google it," the vet warned you,

before I did, and now I interpret
this *rapid unorganized growth*

as one appropriate response
to waking up one day at the edge of the country,
and to the locals' relentless
positivities—a scab on the back of her head

that's blossomed in no time
like everything else in our neighborhood:

Carol's century plant
swelling its already embarrassing stem,
bougainvillea's purple prose
clumped around each TV dish.

2.

If, in my family, you were quiet,
it might mean you were happy. It might

mean that you were angry,
and someone had to find out why,

and if you were angry, in my family,
it might mean that you didn't know yet
(no one knew) you were sad.
That one stayed deepest, lured out
in unwanted lumps

like flaws from a potter's wheel
that spun too fast, but that was its point,
smoothing, covering up.

Anger was a glaze, a way
to present the still-inchoate, set apart

and sealed for the world. My mom
finishing a book a day in bed
the winter she was sick.
My dad cooking soups to freeze.
My brother watching the computer game

over my shoulder, waiting,
in which of those quiets, for his turn.

3.

A four-bore tunnel under brown hills—
when rain falls, it only happens on one side.

It's Tuesday, I'm checking in
with my boss, his shelves besieged with paperbacks
on Church Growth and Leadership.
We never seem to mention God,
but when he speaks of a fog

I recognize it, baffling and reliable
as this afternoon light, the shouts outside,
as kids released from the nursery school
that funds our building
race down the chalked walkway.

Sometimes my baby face
brings others' choices back to them.
So helpless, like dreaming,

the moment he leaves off listening—
(I never should have quit
my church in Boston.
Our friends there, a house downtown . . .)

I'm not losing patience
so much as fearing what regrets I've shared with you
and how talking makes something true
even if it wasn't.

Sundays, I imagine his steps
toward the tall, modernist pulpit
as ice-pick lunges up a cliff:

polar glare reflected everywhere,
engulfing his face.

4.

Outside the cannabis dispensary,
a guard stumps his friend
with the riddle of the Sphinx:

yes, there is a creature
who suffers forms
of such hilarious difference
they sound out of order;

and yes, he must remain one
all that time.

In the display window of Pegasus Books:

Big Nate Lives It Up.
Big Nate Mr. Popularity.
Big Nate Flips Out.
Big Nate In The Zone.
Big Nate Genius Mode.
Big Nate What Could Possibly Go Wrong?

5.

In the noon dream, I'm a tech firm partner,
jeans and blazer, my same age,
announcing his surprise retirement

at the emergency meeting of the board.
He waves his scanner-wand smile
across the tanned angel investors
and Dartmouth buddies

turning suddenly into tables of clergy
and *my* old high school teachers
in their short sleeves and ties,
dark-haired arms crossed, somehow not out of place
among the office scooters and lounge chairs
that overlook the Bay.

Their faces appropriately older,
but crannied with that familiar mix
of authority and sacrifice—
to be here, they must have journeyed far.

Brief stumble, recover. Continue explaining myself
to the window of bright water.
When finally I mention poetry, the front row
can't help grinning at this eccentric
flowering of their influence.

Won over, they surround me,
clenching my right hand with a hint of jealousy
like wedding well-wishers,

distant uncles one understands
one may never see again.

6.

John 20

For Good Friday, your spiritual
director suggested silence

(at least until sundown, when we have plans).
We enforce it like novitiates,
scribbling a note if one goes out,

hearing the foolishness in each missing
reminder or complaint.

You burn votives in the bedroom,
doing something with the Psalms.
I take a Bible and my novel to the window, end up,
like any Friday, trying to write.

On my afternoon jog, crossing the street,
when I see a friend of a friend, I say "Hi"
without thinking. We fall
into walking, up a hill path
I don't know, back past a record shop, a columbarium.
He describes a road in Big Sur

where you and I could park
and sleep unnoticed.

Would faith have been keeping silent
as I would have once,
pretending not to see him?

Succulents like little tusks,
orange asters and impatiens
sparking the sidewalk beds—

which way that we turn
faces our life?

Though afraid, and far from her home,
Mary Magdalene looked.

What she thought had changed, changed twice.

4.

SPIRITUAL PRACTICES

We missed the otter at Big River
but found one later
yards off Highway 1. With glossed snout

it crested up, neck fat slick
as a tourist's, to ponder the lily pads
that festooned the small parking lot pond

while employees of the garden store
poked out to snap pictures.
Someone spoke of a gulch nearby,

an extended drainage pipe,
though the reasons for its arrival
remained as indecipherable

as our own—pulled off in search
of a changing table, now returning to the car
with new shopping in our hands.

"At least she has it to herself," you shrugged.
(One peace lily, dark and lush;
ylang ylang oil in a tiny capsule;

and a bag of donuts
to counteract the mindfulness.)
Buckling our baby in, I followed the restless

torso through the window
as it pulsed rote laps back and forth
like a weather-stranded Olympic swimmer

repeating flip turns
in his motel pool, desperation
held under for the moment

by the familiar violence of his patience.

THE CLOCK OF THE LONG NOW

At the Foundation's bar, called The Interval,
above a Brian Eno *Ambient Painting*
("kaleidoscopic, but never-repeating"),
investors' numbered bottles hang:
lemon, vodka-clear, red-brown.
Along one wall, shelving
stained deep mahogany divides
Futurism from Rigorous Science Fiction,
the collection climbing high
but the spiral stairs roped off.
Weary as a night nurse
charting progress and decline,
the bartender hesitates above
a register's instruction screen, punches
did not like—sent back,
the magnetic card in his hand
swiped downwards hard
like a zipper, or a knife in surgery.
Near the entrance, stools and a counter
encircle the eight-foot Orrery,
prototype of the full-scale clock
designed to last 10,000 years—
a sort of birdcage of iron gears
and colored stones, specially ground
to represent the visible planets
("time's most durable units") in painstaking
revolution. Driven by a bit adder
beneath, and programmed to refresh

twice daily, it hovers and self-alters
silently, the conversation piece
while tourist couples compete for tables.
Is it the inevitable effect
of boredom or ambition to expect,
when our hours and weeks have gone the way
of the *akhet* from ancient Egypt's
calendar, or the Romans' ninth day,
that, scored into remote Nevada limestone,
The Clock of the Long Now
will still be counting something,
still registering and adjusting with the Earth—
that single bead of lazuli,
coolly heroic as it surges
past Saturn's banded onyx, making it
once more around the Sun?

FACE TO FACE

for Zoe May

You first-time snorkeler
head burrowed, missing much
riveted to the fact of water

You literal, now, assemblage of old hopes
hope can sharpen against

When we learned your eyes had unsealed
we stopped telling anyone your names

You spin cycle of sleep and hunger
You moon-print pressure
through the surface of her dress

knocking without asking
crazy for electric bass and basketball crowds

You pressing through
the surface of address

Papaya-sized, once a lemon, once a figment

Hazard to dip
one shoulder lower, then snake yourself
through the straits of bone

You wonder, roughened
You doubt, familiar

Ash swirled down the sky
blew back and forth
when you were just the crooked shelf I'd built
the calendar reminders when to try

Helicopters now
the thrumming almost constant
in Berkeley's raw-glare May

You yard of jewelweeds
you week of circled days

CENTRAL BRANCH

Suitcases, unzipped so they flap,
and knotted Walgreens bags
weighed down at the bottom, like raindrops,

scattered on the classical steps
out of carelessness and enormous faith

Everyone faces the doors
except a woman and girl, her arm
exercising a scooter with purple ribbons
It's a day in the week
It's almost eleven

Swivel-chaired behind the gate
the desk attendant twirls his ID necklace
like a lifeguard's whistle

until ceiling by ceiling
the chilled florescence buzzes on behind him
uncovering the desktop screens
and carrels, the urinals
and *You Are Being Recorded* signs

and in one corner, the new hardcovers
lined up like cereal boxes in a display
for next week's national holiday

INCHWORM AT EMBARCADERO

Where the system map's
metal edge abuts
a fuzzed pink scalp,

an inchworm doubles back,
polite but unrepentant
in sounding the pent-up

space—hides half itself
like an em dash scrunching
to a solemn hyphen,

or a gymnast, all arm
between invisible rings,
or a pawn condemned

to the same two moves,
creative though short-lived,
or the steely tip

on the tuning fork
of a sonometer, twitching,
poised to decipher

the immiserated quiet
that descends (for some
more than others)

when we hit the Transbay
Tube, jolted closer together,
heads worlds away.

LATE AFTERNOON ON SAN PABLO AVE.

Fog pulling down its map of faded lessons.
A last bronze flush
fills the living rooms
of architects and obstetricians in the hills.
Down in the flats,
                           among the candled grottos
of auto shops, a band of tenth-graders drifts,
drunk on their hour of being anyone
after sports, before tutoring.
Who will inform them otherwise?
Not the three along the bar, each two stools apart,
at the Ivy Room, its Dutch door shut
so dust motes stagger
in a lost colony above it.

When the energy-efficient street lights switch on
outside, everyone glances up,
our brows tugged as by a single string.
Noiseless above the intersection, and flat-headed,
like fancy shower nozzles,
their beams stretch a kind of canopy
arcing over the pedestrian island,
the thin man wearing his sandwich board.

The silence of their change is what I think about,
how walking nearby we must have missed it

a hundred times, and won't remember
to look tomorrow, or care.
                              Before I can't
I pull you close, hoping that our hips knock,
awkward and urgent as the high schoolers
who have turned their backs
and rushed to cross against the algorithm.

THREE MONTHS

Gone now the gaping hours
and the question of what counts for work.
Cobwebs older than you

grip the tarry links
on the tandem swing behind the Smart & Final.
We push off again, my giant's fingers
over your still-impossible ones

to keep you from coming back just yet.
Gone the chance, unless in sleep,

to have begun elsewhere,
some equally unlikely confection of moods.
The mounds of woodchips trickle out to grass
at the park's ambiguous limits

where two people in bags are sleeping too,
holding on as carefully
as you, when the commuter trains cross
their rattling winds overhead . . .

Good news creeps up on a face
like a message from another planet,
but in the sly manner of our own daylight.

THE PROOF CLOTH

What she needed most she couldn't stomach much of—
by month four, each dish towel and napkin

in the house, even newly washed, smelled of the milk
she'd gum down hourly, then, smiling wider,

spit back up. As if already she'd caught
her father's penchant for sudden second thoughts.

One afternoon alone, furtive as a teenager,
I slipped one of the cloths inside a Ziploc, sealed

and hid the bag on a shelf in our bedroom closet.
The next day while she slept, small inhalations

could incarnate on demand my favorite inch
of skin between her chin and neck. Judge not. Or judge

that part of love which, when adrenaline
and worry boil off, still wants some remnant, relic,

to itself. Elbows its way among the orthodox
for a glimpse of proof's flimsy fabric.

Tonight, the monitor's grainy military idiom
splays her on her side again, face hidden.

We lay wait in bed, weighing the brief relief
of confirming that she's still breathing

against the catastrophe of her waking up,
and make the incorrect and only choice:

you tiptoe in to check, wool-socked, but the door
still creaks. Accessory, I hang behind

and hear the first cry happening twice,
and watch the tiny animal eyes flare open.

THE CONVERT (II)

after Augustine

Where is it that you go
when I say I've found you,
my mind tricked the right way to look?

Without you, in my lack,
you must've been ahead there, too—
but there is no place like that!

Before my mind learned you,
where else would you have been
but leading me to find you,

moving forward, and then back?
It could have been it was
my mind, tricked the right way to look,

but leading me to find you
without you. In my lack,
when I say I've found you,

where is it that you go?
(You must've been ahead, there, too;
where else would you have been

before?) My mind learned *You*.
Moving forward, and then back—
it could have been. It was.

But there is no place like that.

COURAGE

Stillness until six, the yards and porches
giant toy sets for the street cats.

Each sleep a baffling practice
for leaving you behind
entirely, even if we're touching hands.
For the innocent mind, which it will, wanting out.

Sun re-spreads
among the bungalow façades;
like a memorial on the bank of a river,

shoes in pairs, some children's,
lead to the front doors.

LONELY PLANET

You're used to it, the way,
in the first wide-eyed
minutes, climbing from parking lot
to fire trail, or rifling through
cupboards in a rented kitchen,
I can't help but tell you
we should visit here again,
my reverie inserting
a variation in the season,
or giving friends the room
next door,
                    in stubborn panic
to fix this happiness in place
by escaping from it.
"We're here, now," you'll say,
holding out the book I bought
with its dog-eared maps and lists
and, on the cover, a waterfall,
bright flecks frozen, very close.

Notes

The italicized lines in "Jubilee" come from Leviticus 25.

"Rev. Valentine Rathbun Meets the Shakers" borrows from the account quoted in *The Shakers and the World's People*, edited by Flo Morse.

"Aconite" makes use of Pliny's speculations about the flower in his *Natural History*.

"Impatient Earth" loosely translates Horace's Ode 4.7.

The phrase "Grace is still a secret" is taken from a prose fragment of Emily Dickinson.

The second poem titled "The Convert" is based on a paragraph from Augustine's *Confessions*, Book 10.

Acknowledgments

Thanks to the following journals and anthologies, where some of these poems (sometimes in different forms) appeared: *Best American Poetry 2018, Boston Review, Cincinnati Review, Chicago Review, Dostoevsky Wannabe's Cities: Boston, Free Verse, Harvard Review Online, Hyperallergic, Kenyon Review, The Nation, New York Review of Books, Oversound, Poets.org Poem-A-Day, Poetry Northwest, Prodigal, Raritan, Threepenny Review, Tin House.*

The author wishes to thank Devin Johnston, Kit Novotny, Hai-Dang Phan, Catherine Stearns, Susan Stewart, and Christian Wiman, as well as the James Merrill House, the MacDowell Colony, the Poetry Foundation, and everyone at Princeton University Press, for their support.

PRINCETON SERIES OF CONTEMPORARY POETS